The New Nudity

Hadara Bar-Nadav

Distributed by University Press of New England
Hanover and London

Saturnalia Books
105 Woodside Rd.
Ardmore, PA 19003
info@saturnaliabooks.com

ISBN: 978-0-9899797-2-6
Library of Congress Control Number: 2017937893

Book Design by Richard Every
Printing by McNaughton & Gunn
Cover Art by Ian Francis, *Finally the Future, 20 Years Later*, 2014. Mixed media on panel, 18" x 24".

Author Photo by Sharon Gottula

Distributed by:
University Press of New England
1 Court Street
Lebanon, NH 03766
800-421-1561

My sincere thanks to Henry Israeli, Chris Salerno, and the wonderful staff of Saturnalia Books. Infinite gratitude to Simone Muench and Kevin Prufer, my steady friends and fierce editors. Thanks also to dear friends who have helped me and these poems along the way: Rebecca Morgan Frank, Cyrus Console, Michelle Boisseau, and Steve Paul. Thanks to the University of Missouri-Kansas City and to my bright, inspiring students. Boundless gratitude to my family, endlessly and always. And finally, to my ancestors in the spirit world and to their objects.

Grateful acknowledgment is made to the editors of the following publications in which these poems or versions of these poems first appeared: *AGNI, American Literary Review, Bear Review, Bosque, Cincinnati Review, Columbia Poetry Review, Crazyhorse, Cream City Review, CutBank, Fifth Wednesday, Green Mountains Review, Gulf Coast, The Ilanot Review, Indiana Review, Iowa Review, Kettle Blue Review, Meridian, Mantis, The New Republic, Pleiades, Prairie Schooner, Quarterly West, The Rumpus, Sou'wester,* and *Willow Springs.*

Some of these poems appeared in the chapbook *Fountain and Furnace* (Tupelo Press, 2015), awarded the Sunken Garden Poetry Prize. "Dress (Aurora Borealis)" was awarded the Lucille Medwick Poetry Prize from the Poetry Society of America. "Thumb" was awarded the Lynda Hull Memorial Poetry Prize from *Crazyhorse.* "Swan" was reprinted on *Poetry Daily.*

For my family

In memory of Inge Worth (1923-2016)

Table of Contents

I hear that the axe has flowered ...

> —Paul Celan, "[I hear that the axe has flowered]"

Carnations, those marvelous rags.
How clean they are.

> —Francis Ponge, "The Carnation"

What is the current that makes machinery, that makes it crackle,
what is the current that presents a long line and a necessary waist.
What is this current.

What is the wind, what is it.

> —Gertrude Stein, "A Long Dress"

I.

Thumb

Who means what it is to be human
and is scarred by childhood.

Thick and neckless. Your head shaped
like a gravestone.

A smile opens across the knuckle and disappears
every time you lift a tumbler of scotch.

Who holds a pen and lies.

Who holds a chopstick
in the language of still-twitching fish.

When you think of the past you form a fist
until a heart beats.

Once removed by a chisel. Then reattached.

You stiffen in the rain and dream
of pudding—a smooth, boneless lake.

Who butters morning toast
while wearing a butter hat.

Who fingers the ad for beef, grows numb
while talking to a girl on the phone.

Useless while typing. Useless
tool who only worships space.

A stump. A blackened stamp.
Your own private map of loneliness.

Who always leans to one side. Detached.
Distant from all others.

Fountain

Dirty, dirty boy,
what have you done?

Your bath splattered
with cigarette butts, leaves,

the droppings of doves.

No chlorine can clean
your iron-eating years.

Eyes peeled open,
genitals exposed.

A mounting rod lodged
in the base of your back.

Children poke you
and steal your pennies.

The loose change of your mind
emptied by the smallest hands.

Who isn't barbaric anymore?

The people no longer notice
you, bound in stone,

charming
as a taxidermied swan.

Splayed on the plaza square
in mid-spring,

you wait to be turned on.

Soap

Always a threat
of cleanliness

and its failure
to purify.

      (The showerhead
      shadows my head.)

Rumors of blubber
and human fat.

Troubling histories
hidden

inside the prettiest
pastel cakes.

Swarm of invisible
nibblings.

Foam and its fetish
for the grotesque,

appetite and its pick-
ax smile.

      Secret crevicer

effacing our days,
white-washing injuries.

Even our wounds
become fragrant,

musk and yeast
smelling sickly

      of lavender.

I am afraid
of the drain,

the melt of meat
and ivories,

erasure bubbling up,
rendering us

sweet as
graveyard flowers.

Ladder

Carriage for meat,
the hands and feet.

Cascade
of muddied ribs.

We keep her
locked in the garage

or tied up in the back
of a truck.

Rust among her many colors.

Her shine has gone
nickel-dull.

Blond strands
trapped beneath glue.

Greasy legs
delicate, nicked.

Heels bound
by black rubber.

She steps us closer to God.

The farther we are
from heaven, the more we desire.

Someone opens her,
someone holds her down.

The iron bite of her cry
winds through the streets.

We would not touch
the light any other way.

Door

Hung by two pins and swelling,
lacquered and puckering.

Effaced by thumbprints
sealed with grease and ink.

Your quick hands cancel
my gunmetal locks.

No one notices my head, no one soothes
my forehead with a cool cloth.

You handle me, he handles me.

My gold protuberance
available by turns.

I am legless and cannot move.

I am tongueless, mute
to your touch.

I unleash my deranged triangle
of shadows when pushed.

If you look under my skirt you'll see
the darkness of another world.

Wineglass

You swoon inside a cathedral
of cuts and crush the light in your teeth.

Serrated, furnaced, blown to life
by a drunk man who held you with burned hands.

Blisters pearling each of his fingers
that glossed the surface of your skin.

The most fragile thing:
                    your waist,
        a single strand of rain.

You take merlot into your overgrown mouth,
tongue your walls, and spit.

Your head perfumed with berry
and French oak.

Grown huge and lidless, your eye
becomes a jellyfish glaring back at you.

You are nightly forgotten
on a nightstand

and once collapsed behind
a typewriter, hoping no one could see.

Flush with lust and panting, you hold
your breath like a child until your belly is filled.

Death to the gypsy fruitfly who dares
to steal your drink.

Blood is your one true wish.

Telephone Pole

Blind beacon

who means the death
of green, its petty life.

Is my will to people?

Transmitting
war from house to house.

Chaos rips
through copper,

a haywire noose
tangled around my head.

I once held
the lips of a thousand

sleepy lovers
too far away to meet.

The world become
less strange.

Words for *static*
and *soon*.

Words for *always*
bitten in two.

Years of winter
splintered my throat.

The humming and
the humming.

Your missing
loves return to me

as ghosts with staples
in their mouths.

Drafty wings
on my wires notice me

only as a means
to solicit the sun.

When a man comes
with a drill, I am not

allowed to flinch
but the trembling

hasn't stopped since
I was born.

Spoon

Dimpled by an egg
whose weight vanished.

Where a cloud
once rested its head.

Cradle of the absent
eye, silver socket.

Whose astonishing smoothness
is a torture and an ache.

Who services your hunger
but remains nameless.

Molten memory curls
along the spine.

A furless girl
without arms.

She throws back
her hollow head,

flashes the length
of her singular leg,

clutches her thimble
of milk.

What is taken
cannot be returned.

Her feverish face
dissolving

      at the bottom
      of a pool.

You reach for her first
thing in the morning.

You reach for her
when you cannot sleep,

lulled by her soft
ovals and bells.

House

Ghosts in the attic.
Heaven made of foam.

Pink insulation
unfurling like a gown.

       The (sad) glitter of it.

My love of decay
ever frothing.

Dribbling stucco
witness to the rain.

Sodden soffits.
The wood gone soft.

Slope-shouldered
doorways

       perfectly askew.

Broken down
penny tile like a whole

       mess of bad teeth.

Windows fractured by stars.

Some days only
a squirrel walked by.

Some days only clouds.

Each space occupied
by its dream.

All I ever wanted
was a porch

       I could die on

and a swing whose breeze
would carry me.

Spine

Bone ruffle,

hold up the sky
of myself.

Do not abandon

the body
with your precarious

dress of milk and wire.

Threaded hearts,
barbed ornaments.

26 dumb godlets—

their little skulls
bobbing on the line.

Eyeletted, acid-white.

Mere midden,
             such slippage.

Fear in the fiber,

cloud after
cloud on a string.

            Hello, unraveling.

Torque of dis-
ease, of wince

and prayer. Stay

with me now, stand
next to the spire

of my crumbling.

Chest

The outward form
weighs 125 pounds,

cherry skin
scarred by the sun:

      age spots, knots,
      a darkening figure.

Inside the dead
people live.

Gauze of green
nightgowns.

Mirage of black
and white marriages,

      their glue become
      a yellowed crust

      bubbling beneath
      plastic sheets.

The dead want to rise
from their acid bath.

The dead in shoeboxes,
hatboxes, passports.

The used
and the stamped.

Decades decaying
in tissue paper.

Relentless—
save the rot.

You can save
no one.

The bloodline
blown.

This heaving
heavy empty.

Unpack the casket
of history then

descend
into its red sea.

II.

Pill

You die by drowning
and worship the sea.

Blond anodyne.
Chemical god.

Come quickly,
pool in the blood.

I have been waiting
for you, please,

       insatiable and brittle
       as a chalk-eater.

Promise me a bleach-
clean soul

       and obliteration.

Order the orders,
the hours, the next,

like my family marched
to their shoeless deaths.

Pull your gauze
coverlet over my head.

To sleep finally
in your arms,

smell the snow
on your breath—

I bow to a moon
that fits in my hand.

Diamond

A diamond that hates
diamonds, the dumb

glittering of the self
in the sun.

Glitter during war, glitter
during plague, glittering

      Terezin and electric wire.

Geometry is the enemy
that wounded him

      and pretended it was love.

A head shorn of hair.
The object shorn.

The diamond ran out
of faces, facets, coal,

hidden for years
in the hem of a stolen coat.

I will not trade him for
boots, bread, a passport

or the daughter I lost
singing to herself

on the other side
of the dirt.

Each generation chained,
charred, glittering,

born inside an oven
of roiling earth.

Light siphoned
from my father's bones.

Crown of white fire.

Oven

I live with an oven—
a heavy weight.

I set the timer, trace
its caked corners,

wobble near faint
when considering a square.

Entry. Exit. Door
to nowhere.

Memory framed
by double-paned glass

so I can see the stream
of blue flames caving

the roof of my mouth.

The hiss of history
ablates my face, blisters

my tongue and my name,
numbers me among millions.

I crackle as a leaf.

An entire epoch turned
its face, then washed

its hands for dinner
on an ordinary day.

Who set the table
in silver and lace.

Who closed the door
then opened it.

Box

A dozen voices and
a dozen voices. Lightless.

Their oversized coffin
on wheels.

A giant coffin
in which a hundred voices

and a thousand voices
end. Lightless.

Box and a box
and a box.

House of the dead
still standing.

       Shoulder to shoulder.
       Rib to rib.
       Mouth to emptiness.

A picturesque scene: green
hills, a spotted deer
and her wisp of a fawn.

The open, cloudless sky.

And the giant coffins
trundle by.

Smoke spills
from a whistle's throat.

Metal groans and cries
like a symphony

      crushed underwheel.

A children's game
to count the boxes,

each thundering one
and one and one.

When will it end.
(*End*.)

Coffins for a village
of giants,

cut from their god,
cut from the sky.

Necklace

Dark chain of drool. Silver coil.

Quick noose that severs the starry

        head of each dream.

Tighten and pull. Tighten and pull. Slice clean through.

At the center, a star. A wound.

To whom do I belong? What neck will have me?

Little star whose little heart is an SS death squad.

Each point like a dart—six darts, six knives.

I mark you with my terrible metal smile:

        you are next in line to die.

I burrow into the base of your neck, carve

        away a dimple of bone,

and scent myself with your skin—fear and damp hyacinth.

Gypsy

A birch tree smolders.

No crows to keep her
warm, only flickering.

Sever her arms one
by one. Cut the moths

from their white clot
of heaven.

White mother: breeder
of a million mouths.

Run to the ice cream
truck with your smiles

and wet dimes.
A cherry bomb to suck

and watch the killing
that lasts for days

and stains your lips
a tart red.

The gumball on which
you break a tooth.

The scars of childhood
will not dissolve, searing

your stomach for years,
like the girl who fell

from her bicycle and
kept on falling.

You found her pearl-pale,
lying on the sidewalk,

her head opened,
opening,

like the unborn
gypsy moths, torched

in their white beds.

Sugar

Secret boxes
and bags stashed

in the back
of a never-used oven

or hidden behind pillows
on her smoke-filled settee:

the chocolate cups
and fudge-filled cakes

she numbered
and guarded.

Soil-dark palmfuls
and mouthfuls,

moist and eyeless.

Confections
sweating in plastic,

crowded in the dark
beneath her bed.

Secret sugar
is sweeter and hotter.

Electricity licks
the tongue, a seethe

near suckling
that ruined her mouth.

Dear mother who starved
during the Depression

as rations snatched
her brother away.

Mother who hides
the sugar behind

the spoiled cream
of soft teeth.

Latch

I sense the metal
of you and gush

      under your clamp.

A crushing dream,
blistering pulse.

Salty pressure
beating the blood

      between lipped
      implements.

The god-hold.
Holy seal.

A lunatic's zeal,
unseverable.

Carnivorous, you wrest
my will, pry

      my glandular
      affection.

I break my own
neck to see

your fatted face
erased by hunger,

obscured by
the lavender

      gravity of the moon.

Both of us vanishing
in parts.

      I am siphoned
      by the ounce,

      claimed: udder,
      meat, meal.

Airlessly you lock
and pull.

Your mouth all
steel.

Tongue(less)

A garbage truck drives off
        with my tongue, my drooling girl

dressed in nerve and need
        chattering away in a trash heap.

I missed her when she was still
        at home, snapped pictures of her

in my once-plush bed (memorial
        before the drought), while she slept

twelve hours a day plus a nap after half
        a joint. Now I'm an empty nester.

Now I look in the mirror
        at this erasure, the wasted

gape of my mouth, forsaken
        fount. Now absence rasps

my throat and will not ask
        for pancakes, a pen, or ride

to the dark. My pink child
        has gone for good, hitchhiked

to the city dump. Her big blank
        future, my dry plug of naught.

Each day, a vacant meal.
        There will be no more sentences.

Our books will die in a field.

Bridge

        Wire spokes
through speech.

        Asphalt arches
its back and yawns.

        I don't want
to play the harp

        lashed to signs
and seagulls.

Mouth

I push my mouth
like a small dog

       away from me.

Mongrel, to whom
do you belong?

On the highway we see hair
stripped from skin

pimpled, pale
as spoiled milk,

cows packed
into metal crates on I-80.

Their mouths are slack,
prepped for slaughter

in splattered factories
in Lincoln and Des Moines.

My mouth pouts
in the back seat

and weeps, an icepick
turning inside my mind.

We are all in pieces,

sad we are not Picasso
who could make beauty

from *a horde of destructions.*

Other trucks drive by,
this time carting

pigs, then horses,
then people.

People stuffed
into crates—

       reaching for rain
       through the slats.

They did not want
their mouths either,

hungry and crying,
hiccupping black air,

their tireless need
to announce

themselves like
clamorous children

who want and
want. And wail.

Dress (Aurora Borealis)

See me for miles—

    lightstreaked,
    deathstreaked.

A disturbance.
(I am disturbed.)

    Theatrical
    and skinless.

    Electrical, all
    edge.

A knife of ice
carving the sky.

White blades,
white fathom,

    unbridled.

White that is red
is pink is hue

    is glazed enormity,
    tangerine plush.

And then comes
the blood,

    scarlets on fire.

Why is a girl always
on fire.

What makes her
crackle—

     breathtaking,
     the cut waist,

     thighs rushed
     by smoke,

     roil of voile,
     combustible.

So I loved, laid, slept
for days, blinked,

breathed flame,
paraded like a god.

Gianter than god
and vincible.

     Made of nothing at all.

     Fleshless,
     a fuse of refusals.

And am I beautiful
now, who owns beauty,

waiting for your tongues
to slip by.

III.

Leg

She must be French,

a deco dream
dimpled, curved.

Candled,
a rose glow.

Her soft golds
golding.

The new nudity
drives attention.

Arches of light—

      calligraphic.

Ankle bone cut
like a jewel.

What is a knee for,
and so she kneels.

Pulse and pulley

      breaking and
      unbreaking the lines.

Quick horse
of the torso

     and glide.

Most fleet
sweetness.

Swift carriage
exceeding

     its gilded shape.

Her form kicks
free of the frame.

Match

I remain your sweet
        erratic, your eviscerated

wind who records every
        leaving. This is hovering

now feel my high
        heel on your lip?

I will not be
        embodied, fingerprints

on the doorknob and the scrape
        of click. A siren sears

far then near, smoke
        catches your fire escape.

Fire, fire, fire.

        I'll be your match-
blackened weather.

Tweezer

I could kill a man.

Swallow hard and tempt me
to slash the Adam's apple—

     voicebox blown
     open like a rose.

Could I have spared him,

     excised the scourge,
     the dirty blood

     (spirochetes
     seethe in cavities).

I am forever
severed, two-headed.

     Merciless. Mercurial.

Blood flows from the fatted
trunk of a tick—

     a female pulled fully
     formed from your thigh.

I extract your excess,
widen your wound,

entranced by
the barbed bite.

Blunt heart
of a butcher.

We all eat and eat
and eat—

the flesh,
a red harvest.

Jar

Home was a jar,
glassy and tight,

airless as the inside
of a balloon.

     All blur, all melt.

We drifted through blue-
lit rooms in the basement

like boneless bats
distorted, stretched

around racks of
smoke and hunger.

The ashtrays always
full, mounds

     of scarred breath,
     the torture of clouds.

Nodding away
whole afternoons.

     Decembering—the lure
     and pull of null.

We sealed ourselves
in, afraid of vanishing

if we left and we
were vanishing.

Glazed, numbed,
high as

      chandeliers and silence.

A bliss that was
blistering.

Night

In couplets one expects a couple
in a tree. Birds scribble

    their fury across the sky.

Say *sky* here and blue opens.
Say *black* and night throws its drink.

The sky reminds us of an invitation
elsewhere. Even a storm has its charm.

Who can complain about the sky
when we have each other?

If there is a hand in the sky.
If we had a hand in it.

The sky feeds itself to itself, a furnace
of copper and blood.

The sky drops its aluminum eye,
rolls its grief in ink.

Who are we, sky of reflection,
who wince, who weep?

The night is a lake of needles.

    The night, a field of teeth.

The sky burns overhead
or the sky falls and buries us.

Table, Bed, Violin

Nothing is the right size or shape
        but we are in love so the damage
        charms us. In the flooding world we wave

goodbye to the table that let us rest
        our dinner plates and our heads,
        a good table rising up as if walking

away. Goodbye mattress who cradled us,
        carrying us across miles of mud-
        crusted dreams before buckling

and tossing itself into the sea. Goodbye
        violin who cupped my chin, filled
        my ears, and held me. Such fullness

too much for one small home, so she sails
        off with her timbre and horsehair.
        The couch is only a pencil sketch

but has promised to stay. We drink
        our silt with wine, recall the wayward
        waters that left us behind.

Balcony

Who spends her whole life kneeling
on metal slats and rain.

Ladder for dalliances and thieves.

Of hanging, being hung, of steel
teeth forked into a brick wall.

Of battery, blistering,
canopy, tarp, and leaking.

Of abandoned nests and spider legs,
the ashen arms of ferns.

Solitary days, touchless nights.

The fire escapes itself,
the fire never arrives.

Witness of stunted
vistas and hashmarks of light.

Of the dull routine of kitchens
and incessant televisions.

Of a woman dancing in a bra and a man
rubbing the stump of his leg.

Of a tragic daughter put out to dry.

Cage of wrong angles, clanging
her fear of heights.

Of momentary friendships with
the drift of yellow leaves

and ten-minute love scenes
with barefoot strangers.

Ribboned by strands of miniature stars.

The moon illuminates each rusted bar
and cuts her world to pieces.

Of the slow darkness, always
suspended, always falling.

Of the burden of exile
and snow, the verbless present—.

Blue

And you are full
of winking.

A convex ceiling
blistered. Riddled.

Some call you god
and light the flames

      of their throats.

Men sigh
their little clouds.

Hours of last requests.

The moon throws shade
over the vacant

host and all
the romantical corpses,

      husks of clove and rot.

Wind burns its way
through the cracks.

You, the surround
and inbound:

veins flowing
into sky,

sea falling
into a mind of midnight.

Phlox, acacia,
some pretty things

blue-lipped,

that beat the right
side of your brow.

Watch

A watch has sawed off
my ear, lodged its steel body
in place, tearing my jaw a little,

unzippering my neck. A watch
that watches me, that ticks
its tiny blades, that tocks

and has no heart. Gears crimp and
scissor the air, the days, the years,
the arms that never stop. Hear

each second chipping away, flaying
itself. Hear it radiate through the bell
of my skull, down the hallway

of my throat. Each tooth ticks,
yellows, chips. Even my dog
hears it. She will not come

to me, does not trust my broken
smile, my shaking hands.
Now she sleeps in the garden

by the mute lilacs and half-dead oak,
but I have no escape. When I wake
the watch is already awake,

waiting. It never quickens or slows
as I walk quickly or slowly to the mailbox
or Vidler's Store to buy razor blades,

turpentine, or paint. It takes me
everywhere, or I take it,
my constant ache, my constant.

Plant

Who is no one's pet and
will not be touched. Ever.

The great immovable
passed out in a window.

Unwell and unwelcomed,
forgotten guest.

Once gift and gorgeous,
emerald, all jewel.

From the start
a volatile symbol.

Hello exchanged for love
or *hello* for death,

the plant cannot remember

who wished or lost
or wore a veil of dust,

such moist occasions
and departures.

She drinks and dulls
all afternoon

and drops her many
heart-shaped heads,

leathered by the sun
that mothers

and kills, forever
tied to her grave.

Swan

Sail
of surrender.

Cold geometry.

Slow ice treading
on blue skin.

Slow dread

       (treading, treading).

Beauty as a form
of isolation,

       bled and tethered.

An accidental hook
rusted in.

She dreams of green
meat and eel grass,

a blizzard of fireflies,

but survives on air
and decay.

Winded instrument
that sings

about drowning
under a pale awning.

Her cry stripped
of its chord,

a wounded call
that will not carry.

Sludge inside
her shining—

swirls of
opalescent oil.

Each circle rings
then shatters

then violetly
disappears.

A flock of zeros
follows her everywhere,

unslakable and damaged.

Carved angel,
chimerical,

a cold melt.

Death dressed
in snow.

IV.

Shadow

Take two Percocet
and dissolve.

One is ever haunted.

A dark sea, a season
of ghosts

splashing on the blue wind.

The night dragging
behind us.

Light, the enemy,
dark, the enemy,

who will never shine.

The other face that shivers
beneath each leaf,

daughter of awnings.

She arrives late to dinner
always carting a façade,

drinks all the scotch
in the cabinet,

walks into walls
and grows strange.

Diabolical silhouette
with a tusk and a huge head.

She inhales entire rooms,
claims every crevice,

straddles the bed
and violates sleep.

A black thought

caught between the eyelid
and the eye.

Sun

Blistered apple,
gold that molts

the eye & boils
animals in their caves.

I touch & touch

       & touch,

branding the hands
of each child.

A circle
of unmoored fury.

I see death all
around you—

       your phantomed self
       charred blue,

       cast against
       asphalt.

The body's ash already
visible,

       unglittering
       in its cheap velvet.

Bow down
in the brilliance

    of your borrowed light.

Let me ignite
your end.

Page

Do not look
up from the one

      tiny mark.

Scare, scar, mar
of it across

      the black irides.

Not even tree,
but its pulped failure.

Space for charting
error's ink-

      dipped slurs.

Sloppy sutures
in milk.

The mind slips,

      shucked loose,

and all the words
for meaning

crushing down,
sheeting the head

in hospital-white.

I inherited this blighted
alphabet—

pale palette of ice

crosshatched
by minuses and arrows.

Lung

Open your little white
flutterings.

Paper frills
that will not take flight.

A cluster of scars.

Carnations withering
about the face.

Disintegrating lace
occupied by winter.

Mouthsacks shredded
by their song.

Show me the gray
root of ruin.

The broken kite
of your chest.

Once, *the organ
of air,*

                of light.

But the metaphors
fail.

You will not rise.

Pigeon

A whistle trembles
beneath each wing,

      strange music

without message
or mouth,

known only
by the wind.

You are become
my father of bent

      syntax and ash.

A whittled
heart, mud-colored.

You haunt
the horizon, cling

to wires overhead
and watch.

Ghosts gather
along the lines.

Multiples multiply.
(Which pigeon is mine?)

Little blades of slate,
gunmetal, lead.

I lose you in the great
green head of an oak.

Even loss is
lost and radiates,

its liquid
shadow falls

      across the earth.

Nail

Sink the slip
of light.

Box the night
where it breeds.

Rivet the pine

      (coffin, coffin).

Autopsy of then
punctured, husked.

      You make a little
      wind,

      breath
      cut by hand.

And then the mindless
splintering, mindlessly.

      Connector
      who unbuilds a house.

      Dismantler
      who fixes the dark.

Contain
this wooden end.

Man as memory
pinned

beneath the wolf
of your tooth.

Heart

A bad word
in a poem, smutmouth.

Now wipe the shine
from your lips.

Bordeaux-soaked impulse
murmuring below speech.

You sound like
a limp,

a little ghost
and its echo.

You touch every dead part,
even the toes, farthest
from God.

Hospitals of blood
lie sleepless
in your caverns.

Even tucked inside
the darkness of the body
you will not last.

Quiver of jelly
that collapses a life.

You stole my father
in his sleep.

Flayed fist of twitches
bursting, bound.

Servant with numerous
incisions.

Master
with too many mouths.

A furnace of tongues.

Press your ear
to the wound.

Here the dead sing.

Piano

Animal bent
by a cage.

      Lion at the knees.

Song of bone
and wire.

Death on the wires.

      The hands always hanging there—

An angular throat,
throat like a wing.

A note held and held.

Music
as it vanishes.

Sheet

What contains
and cancels

      the strange, still body.

Veil, shroud, shred.

Scratch of fabric
that roars.

Drape the mirrors
so you will not see

      your seeing,

so form disappears.

Pain of plain
linen.

Your eyes closed.
(My eyes closed.)

Cool cheek down
on the sheet (page),

      color of a blizzard.

You will end all
of your days here

(I will end all
of my days here)

in this blinding god-
forsaken field.

Feather

Broken machine.

A part abandoned
by its purpose.

The glorious verb
you were.

Torn away, from,
ever.

Your brief home
of air and astonishment

(hushed astronomy).

No clawing after,
no hesitation as you fall.

Misshapen pinwheel
spiked with hair.

Fringes dead and teeming.

Infested shred
of your former self.

The dovecote rejects you.

Without a heart
you do not belong.

The grass flares
its million needles.

Grief crowing overhead.

Who knows the wind
will no longer carry you

or softly set you down.

Who knows every wind
is hard.

Hooklets unhooked,
barbs bent,

vanes that know
no direction.

Your point chewed
off so you can

no longer dream
of drafting

volumes or demand
an audience

for your staggering
descent.

Epic falter,
little feather,

figment
of cough and thread.

Wind (Elegy)

Red hollow,
red howl—

    (though I am not supposed
    to say such words)

blood words
that illuminate

the empty anchor
of air you are.

Nameless hurricane.
Windcrush.

Late lament

    lost in noise.

Sear. Sever.
The never again.

    Without lilies
    or balm,

    without a wish
    for better

    or a childhood song.

Ur-alphabet
gurgling undertongue

where God sculpts
his voids.

Worm

Spiny-headed and spiny-crowned,
hook and round,

acorn, peanut, phallus, velvet,
goblet, jaw, ribbon, tongue,

the tape and the flat,
and, finally, the segment—

Annelida of the Ganglia,
Grand Dame of Dirt,

hermaphrodite of nerves
and love, with her vine

of five hearts and will to woo,
who touches us all at last.

Zombie

A zombie is a head
with a hole in it.

Layers of plastic,
putty, and crust.

The mindless
must be sated.

Mottled men who will
always return

        mouthing wet
        promises.

You rise already
harmed and follow

        my sad circle

as if dancing
on shattered legs.

Shoeless, toeless,
such tender absences.

You come to me
ripped

        in linens and reds,

eternal, autumnal
with rust and wonder.

My servant, sublimate
and I am yours

(the hot death
we would give each other).

My dark ardor,
my dark augur.

Love to the very open-
mouthed end.

We are made of
so much hunger.

Notes

"Dress (Aurora Borealis)" was inspired by Ambreen Riasat, a victim of an "honor killing" on April 29, 2016. Thirteen people, including some of her own family members, were arrested in connection to her murder.

"Leg" is after Egon Schiele's *Reclining Female Nude with Violet Stockings*.

"Table, Bed, Violin" is after René Magritte's *Landscape with Table, Bed, Violin*.

"Nail" is after René Magritte's *The Balcony*.

The New Nudity is a phrase adapted from Spencer Reece's *The Clerk's Tale* (Houghton Mifflin, 2004).